T0321284

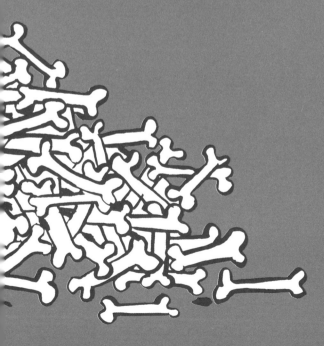

This book is dedicated to Marina Abramović and to Grandma Bruna. —FG

Phaidon Press Inc.
111 Broadway,
New York, NY 10006

Phaidon Press Limited
2 Cooperage Yard
London, E15 2QR

phaidon.com

This edition © 2024 Phaidon Press Limited
First published as *Marina Abramović* by Fausto Gilberti
© Fausto Gilberti, © Maurizio Corraini s.r.l.
Published by arrangement with Maurizio Corraini s.r.l.

Text set in Raisonne Demibold and Fugue Regular

ISBN 978 1 83866 882 2
006-0724

Printed in China

List of the works and performances in this book, Courtesy of the Marina Abramović Archives

p15 "Freeing the Memory", performance, 90 min., Dacić Gallery, Tübingen, 1975. © Marina Abramović
p16–17 "Art Must Be Beautiful, Artist Must Be Beautiful", performance, 60 min., Copenaghen, 1975. © Marina Abramović
p18–19 "Rhythm 0", performance, 6 hours, Studio Morra, Napoli, 1974. © Marina Abramović
p20–21 "Imponderabilia", with Ulay, performance, 90 min., Galleria Comunale d'Arte Moderna, Bologna, 1977. © Ulay / Marina Abramović
p22–23 "Relation in time", with Ulay, performance, 17 hours, Studio G7, Bologna, 1977. © Ulay and Marina Abramović
p24–25 "AAA-AAA", with Ulay, performance, 15 min., Liège, February 1978. © Ulay / Marina Abramović
p26–27 "The Lovers", with Ulay, performance, 90 days, Great Wall of China, March–June 1988. © Marina Abramović and Ulay
p28–29 "Shoes for Departure", Amethyst crystal, 1991-2015. © Marina Abramović
p30–31 "Balkan Baroque", performance, 4 days and 6 hours, XLVII Biennale d'Arte di Venezia, June 1997. © Marina Abramović
p32–35 Abramović Method, carried out by her institute, MAI (Marina Abramović Institute)
p36–45 "The Artist Is Present", performance, 3 months, Museum of Modern Art, New York, March–May 2010. © Marina Abramović
p48 Photo credit: Marco Anelli, Courtesy of the Marina Abramović Archives

MARINA ABRAMOVIĆ

Turned Herself Into Art and Wasn't Sorry.

Fausto Gilberti

My name is Marina.

Before I tell you my story, will you close
your eyes with me for a moment?

How does your body feel? Where does
your imagination take you?

I think about these things when I make art.

I grew up in a European country called Yugoslavia,
which doesn't exist anymore. When I was young, religious
holidays like Christmas weren't allowed there.

But my Grandma Milica was very religious, so we celebrated
in secret by pulling dark curtains across the windows.

Ssshhhh!

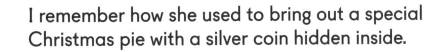

I remember how she used to bring out a special Christmas pie with a silver coin hidden inside.

Whoever found that coin would be lucky for a year!

Grandma Milica was kind, brave, and gave me big kisses that helped me feel safe and calm.

She lit candles to pray every day. I loved this and I loved her. She lived to 103.

I never got kisses from my mother. She was tough and had lots of rules. I couldn't play on the swing, or with friends, or look messy — even in bed, when I was asleep!

But my mother made sure I learned many things, including music and art, which I loved.

My father and I had fun together. He was great
at surprises! One of the best was when he asked
an artist friend of his to give me a painting lesson.

The artist threw some paint and sand on a canvas,
and set fire to it!

"It's a sunset," he told me.

His performance was so memorable that I decided
to hang the blackened canvas on my bedroom wall.

I knew I would be an artist one day. At home I had
my own studio where I could paint. When I was little,
I painted flowers. Then, I painted my dreams.
When I was a bit older, I painted clouds.

I loved watching clouds. I tried to guess what shapes
they made in the sky.

One cloudless day, I saw planes fly over, leaving behind beautiful white trails high above me. I watched them slowly vanish until the sky was a perfect blue again . . .

Then, I had an idea! I wanted to make my own drawings in the sky. I went to the nearby air base and asked if they would fly their planes for me.

. . . Unfortunately, I never got planes to draw with, but that day I discovered something important: I could make art from *anything* around me! Even things that moved and changed, like fire, water, sounds . . . my own body! *I* could be art!

I stopped painting pictures and started PERFORMING, turning myself into art, in front of people. I was a performance artist!

Suddenly I felt free.

I began exploring what my body could do.

Once, I spoke every word that came into my head until my mind became empty.

Another time, I brushed my hair fiercely while saying the same words, over and over, for an hour.

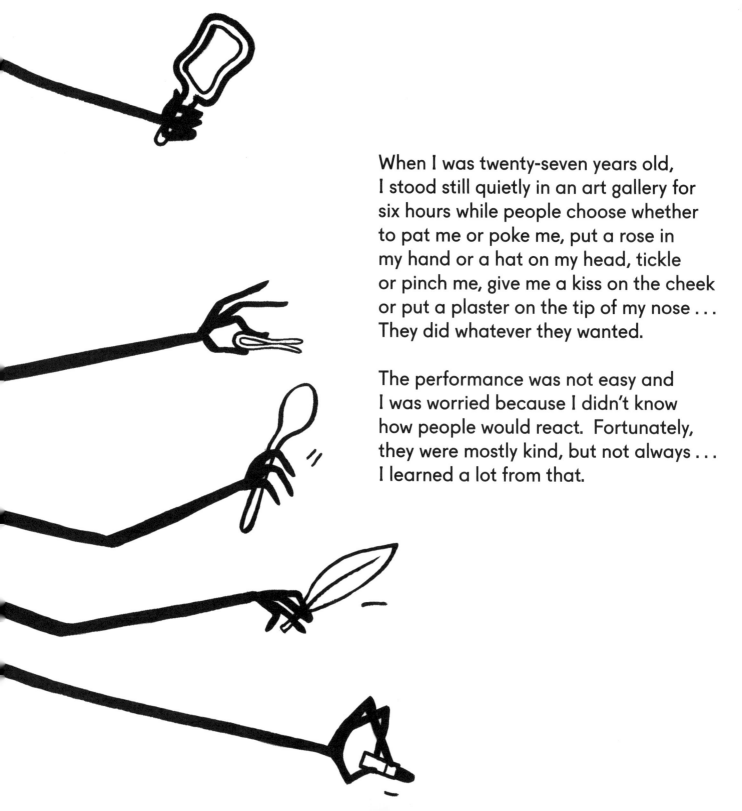

When I was twenty-seven years old,
I stood still quietly in an art gallery for
six hours while people choose whether
to pat me or poke me, put a rose in
my hand or a hat on my head, tickle
or pinch me, give me a kiss on the cheek
or put a plaster on the tip of my nose . . .
They did whatever they wanted.

The performance was not easy and
I was worried because I didn't know
how people would react. Fortunately,
they were mostly kind, but not always . . .
I learned a lot from that.

A year later, I met Ulay. He was an artist like me. We fell in love and began to travel around Europe, working hard and sleeping in a van.

At one of our first performances, we stood facing each other, very close together and naked at the entrance to the Museum of Modern Art in Bologna, Italy. To get through the door, people had to squeeze between us.

We wanted to see their reactions.

Not everyone dared to go through!

Ulay and I both had long hair, and one day
we tied our ponytails together.

We sat back-to-back for seventeen hours,
trying not to pull each other's hair.

Then there was the time we screamed into each other's faces until one of us lost their voice.

I don't remember whose voice went first, but it doesn't matter because it wasn't a competition . . .

. . . Or was it?

One day, Ulay and I decided it was time to go
our separate ways. As a final performance together,
we walked the very long Great Wall of China
from two opposite ends.

We walked for three whole months until we met
in the middle, tired and with our shoes worn bare.

Then we hugged each other tightly and said goodbye.

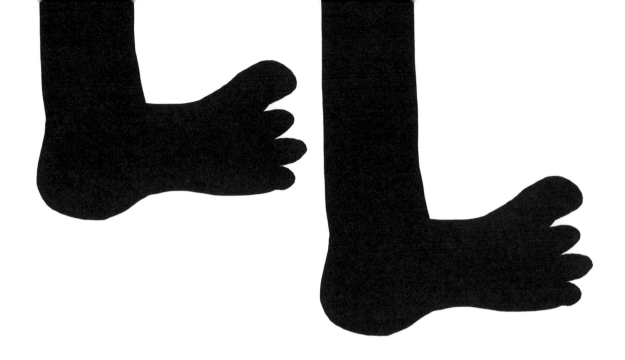

Back home, I thought of the rocks beneath my feet
on that walk.

I made two enormous shoes out of amethyst rock.
They were big enough to fit a giant! Anyone who
wore them could set off on a magical journey.

Of course, it would be an imaginary journey because
the shoes were far too heavy to walk in!

It was around this time that Yugoslavia, my home country, went to war. I wasn't living there, but I felt it deeply. It took me years to find a way to express the sadness and shame.

Then I did it — in a performance at the famous Venice Biennale art festival.

For four days, I sat on a mountain of cow bones, scrubbing them while singing folk songs from my childhood.

It was very hot that summer and the bones began to smell.

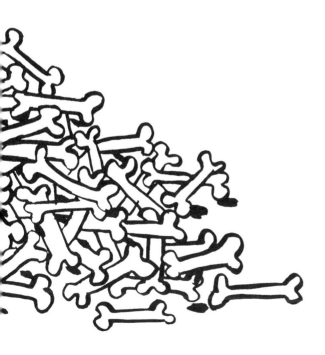

After that performance, people recognized me more.
Sometimes they would stop me in the streets, as if I were
a movie star. I went around the world teaching art students
ways to free their mind and be more creative.

I designed bright cone hats, with magnets. Balancing them on
our heads was challenging, but concentrating gave us energy.

Other times, we would lay still with our eyes closed, just
breathing and feeling our bodies . . .

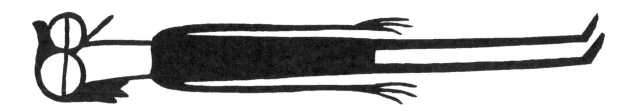

. . . and hug trees or count grains of rice for hours.

We would walk backwards, or blindfolded.

All these things gave us strength — the kind that helps us keep going in difficult times.

I needed this strength more than ever, for a very special performance . . .

I set up two chairs and a table at the Museum
of Modern Art in New York City. I sat in one
of those chairs and closed my eyes.

When someone sat down opposite me,
I opened my eyes. We weren't allowed
to speak or touch, just look.

The performance was called *The Artist is Present*.

People waited to sit with me, day after day. They stayed for as long as they wanted. Some people left after just a few minutes, while others gazed at me for many hours.

I sat still as a statue, six days a week for three months, and locked eyes with 1,545 people.

I saw peace, joy, fear, anger, pain, and hope in their eyes.

Some of them smiled at me. Others wept tears. Someone pulled funny faces.

I was like a mirror, reflecting people's emotions.
We seemed to talk to each other without words.

I turned myself into art, and I wasn't sorry. Even though it wasn't easy, sitting there all day without eating, drinking, stretching, or going to the toilet.

I made my own rules and only broke them once, when I opened my eyes to find a face I hadn't seen for more than twenty years.

I leaned forward and took Ulay's hands in mine.

By the time I finished *The Artist is Present*,
my neck, back, arms, and bum ached!

My mind was exhausted, and my eyes were
sore. But I also felt happy and alive.

I sat still for so long, but at the same time,
I took a journey.

A wonderful journey through many emotions.

MORE ABOUT MARINA ABRAMOVIĆ

Marina Abramović was born in 1946, in the European country that used to be Yugoslavia. Her parents were busy working, so until she was six, Marina lived with her grandmother. She loved her grandmother and her religious rituals, which later inspired her art. But when she moved back home, her parents were often fighting and her mother was extremely strict.

Marina took comfort in painting. She had her own art studio at home. She painted and painted until one day in her teens, she saw some planes "drawing" trails in the sky. Marina realized she could make art from anything! She went to art school and started performing. She liked to put herself in difficult situations to test the limits of her body and see how others would react.

When Marina met Ulay, they worked together, performing artworks that needed lots of trust and strength. They planned to get married after walking the Great Wall of China from opposite ends, but when they met in the middle, they split up instead.

Marina became world famous, both performing and showing people ways to focus their mind and energy in the moment. She trained for over a year for *The Artist is Present*, saying how hard it is to do almost nothing. Today she still works and teaches artists to perform using her Abramović Method. In this way, she keeps on sharing her journey with art lovers all around the world.

Marina Abramović performed *The Artist Is Present* in 2010, at the Museum of Modern Art in New York. She sat still for 3 months (716.5 hours to be exact). Nearly a million people came to see her show, and 1,545 of them sat in the chair opposite her.

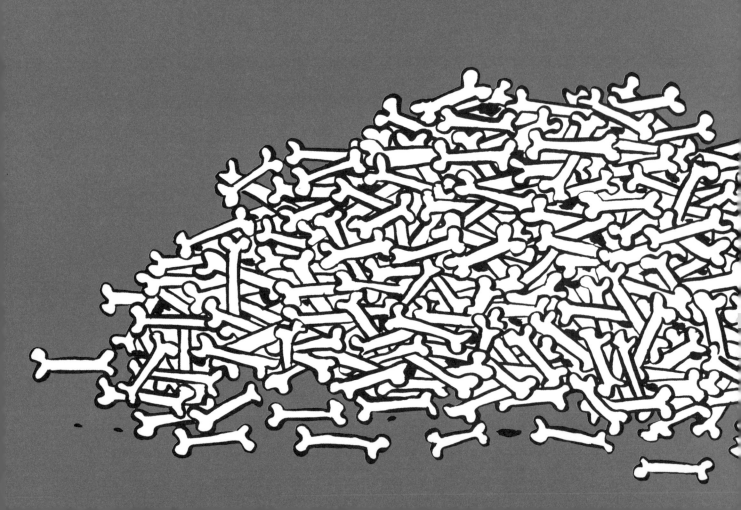